ON THE RUN
True Stories of Legendary Outlaws

The Story of
BONNIE AND CLYDE

LINDSEY LOWE

T0054321

Enslow
PUBLISHING

Published in 2024 by Enslow Publishing, LLC
2544 Clinton Street
Buffalo, NY 14224

Copyright © 2023 Brown Bear Books Ltd

Portions of this work were originally authored by Tim Cooke and published as *Bonnie and Clyde*.
All new material in this edition are authored by Lindsey Lowe.

Children's Publisher: Anne O'Daly
Design Manager: Keith Davis
Designer: Lynne Ross
Picture Manager: Sophie Mortimer

All rights reserved. No part of this book may be reproduced
in any form without permission in writing from the publisher, except by a reviewer.

Manufactured in the United States of America

CPSIA compliance information: Batch #CSENS24: For further information contact
Enslow Publishing LLC, New York, New York at 1-800-398-2504.

Please visit our website, www.enslowpublishing.com. For a free color catalog of all our high-quality books,
call toll free 1-800-398-2504 or fax 1-877-980-4454.

Cataloging-in-Publication Data

Names: Lowe, Lindsey.
Title: The story of Bonnie and Clyde / Lindsey Lowe.
Description: New York: Enslow Publishing, 2024. | Series: On the run: true stories of legendary outlaws |
Includes glossary and index.
Identifiers: ISBN 9781978536685 (pbk.) | ISBN 9781978536692 (library bound) | ISBN 9781978536708 (ebook)
Subjects: Barrow, Clyde, 1909-1934—Juvenile literature. | Parker, Bonnie, 1910-1934—Juvenile literature. |
Criminals—United States—Biography—Juvenile literature.| Bank robberies—United States—History—20th
century—Juvenile literature.
Classification: LCC HV6785.C66 2024 | 364.15'52092273—dc23

Picture Credits
Front Cover: Library of Congress.
Alamy: Everett Collection Historical 26, John Frost Newspapers 41; Backgate: 30; Dallas Police
Department: 8, 31; Dreamstime: Kathryn Sidenstricker 21; FBI: 17, 25, 28, 39, 45; Forgotten Weapons: 9;
IFCAR: 16; Library of Congress: 4,5, 7, 10, 11, 12, 20, 27, 33, 35; National Archives: 13, 18, 22, 23, 29, 44;
Robert Hunt Library: 42; Shutterstock: 4, Everett Historical 40; TexasHideout Tripod: 36, 37; Thinkstock:
James Steidl 15; Topfoto: AP 32, The Granger Collection 24, 34;
Vanessa E. Zekowitz: 19; Warner Bros. Seven Arts: 43.

All other artwork/maps Brown Bear Books

Find us on

CONTENTS

INTRODUCTION

Bonnie and Clyde were famous outlaws in the early 1930s. They robbed gas stations, stores, and banks, and killed anyone who tried to stop them.

In October 1929, New Yorkers gathered near the Stock Exchange on Wall Street. They were worried about their savings.

To begin with, some people thought Bonnie Parker and Clyde Barrow were heroes. In the 1930s, life in the United States was hard. There had been an economic crash. Firms closed and many people lost their jobs. People were poor. When Bonnie and Clyde started to rob banks many people thought they were fighting against poverty. That view of the outlaws soon changed. Bonnie and Clyde's gang shot dead at least nine police officers. They also killed civilians. People turned against them and the gang then spent most of its time on the run from the law.

Growing up in a boom

Bonnie and Clyde were teenagers in the 1920s. The United States experienced an economic boom. It was an exciting time. There were plenty of jobs. The country's wealth increased. Many Americans had money to buy new goods, such as radios and automobiles. Life for women had changed dramatically. The symbol of the modern woman was the flapper. These young women had bobbed haircuts, wore shorter skirts, and were independent. Many also had jobs for the first time.

The flappers were considered to be daring young women. They looked modern. They cut their hair short and wore skirts that revealed their legs.

The bust

The economic boom of the 1920s was too good to last. People and banks invested money in the stock market. In 1929, the stock market suddenly lost all its value. The economy collapsed. People rushed to take their money out of the banks. By 1933, 4,000 banks had closed. Millions of people lost their life savings. Unemployment in the cities rocketed as companies went bust. Things were no better in the countryside. Large parts of the Midwest turned into a dust bowl. The soil dried up and blew away in the wind. Crops failed and families starved. Desperate people drifted across the country looking for work. The period was called the Great Depression.

Feeling of betrayal

Most Americans felt betrayed by the government. Many men had fought against the Germans in World War I (1914–1918). They came home from the war hoping for a secure future. They believed that if they worked hard and saved money, they would be able to live well. The Depression crushed

This sculpture in Washington, D.C., shows unemployed men standing in line waiting for food during the Great Depression.

Poor, unemployed men looking for work in the Great Depression walk past a billboard from the boom years that advises taking the train.

their hopes. In the same way, many women had enjoyed being able to work in the 1920s. Now jobs were scarce, and women found themselves stuck at home again.

Bonnie Parker and Clyde Barrow were young adults when the Great Depression started. They faced difficult futures and made a choice. They decided to embark upon a life of crime.

A Poor Start in Life

Clyde Barrow's childhood was not a happy one. His family was extremely poor. Clyde soon turned to crime.

Clyde Barrow was born on March 24, 1909, in Texas. His family was very poor. In the early 1920s they lived in West Dallas. At the time the neighborhood was a run-down area. The family had so little money they had to live under their station wagon while they saved to buy a tent.

Clyde's first incident with the law came when he was 17 years old. He rented a car and did not return it, so he was arrested. He found a number of jobs, but he began to steal cars and rob stores to

These police photographs show Clyde Barrow in 1926, when he was first arrested. He was 17 years old.

add to his small wage. Clyde was arrested several times. In April 1930 he was sent to Eastham Prison Farm. The prison had a reputation as being a tough, brutal place.

A bitter criminal

Clyde was released from jail in February 1932. He was no longer a minor criminal. He had become a murderer. While he was in jail, Clyde had killed his cellmate, "Big Ed" Crowder. Crowder had assaulted Clyde. Clyde smashed his skull with a lead pipe.

On his release, Clyde formed the Barrow Gang. They began robbing small grocery stores and gas stations. Clyde carried a Browning automatic rifle. He blamed the authorities at Eastham Prison for his mistreatment by Crowder and threatened to take revenge on the prison.

A DIFFERENT PERSONALITY

People who knew Clyde said his experiences in Eastham changed him. The guards did not protect him from Ed Crowder, who assaulted him often. When he was released, his sisters said his character had changed so much they barely recognized him. Another prisoner said Clyde had become a "rattlesnake."

Clyde carried an M1918 Browning Automatic Rifle. It had been designed for use by soldiers in World War I.

Life on Prison Farms

In Texas, the state government had many prison farms. They were tough places, and Eastham Prison Farm was one of the worst.

After the end of the Civil War (1861–1865), the Southern states that had joined the Confederacy suffered from a high level of crime. There was also a lack of money. In Texas, the state could not afford to keep all its criminals in prison. To solve the problem, the state government hired out prisoners to private companies as workers. The prisoners worked during the day in mines or on railroads or plantations.

Prison farms

The hiring out of prisoners was finally abolished in 1910. Instead, Texas started to buy plantations

A prison warden (right) and two guards stand inside a Texas prison in the early 20th century.

and farms. By 1921, state prison farms covered more than 81,000 acres (33 ha). They did not make any money, but the state used the prison farms as a form of punishment. The Eastham Prison Farm in Huntsville, where Clyde Barrow was sent, was where Texas sent its toughest prisoners. They harvested cotton under the blazing Texan sun. It was hard, physical work.

CONDITIONS IN THE PRISON

Living conditions for prisoners on the prison farms were poor. The cells were filthy and full of rats and insects. The guards were tough and often treated the prisoners badly. Violence between the prisoners was common. The guards ignored unexplained deaths among the prisoners.

Meeting Bonnie

Clyde met Bonnie in West Dallas in January 1930. It was love at first sight, but shortly afterward, Clyde was sent to prison.

Bonnie Parker was born on October 1, 1910, in Rowena, Texas. Her father died when she was four years old, and her mother took Bonnie and her brother and sister to live with their grandparents in a poor area of Dallas known as "Cement City." Today it is part of West Dallas.

By the time she met Clyde Barrow, Bonnie was already married. She had dropped out of school to marry Roy Thornton on September 25, 1926. She was only 15 years old. The marriage was not happy. The couple separated, but never divorced. Thornton was later sent to prison for murder.

This is downtown Dallas around 1930. Bonnie and Clyde lived in West Dallas, a poorer part of the city.

A MODERN WOMAN?

Some historians think Bonnie is the real reason Bonnie and Clyde became so popular. They say that Clyde was a lazy, violent criminal. But they describe Bonnie as a tough, independent woman. She tried to make the best of her life, and she always stood by Clyde in times of trouble.

Bonnie and Clyde lived as a married couple, even though Bonnie was already married.

A talent for poetry

Bonnie worked as a waitress in a diner, but she lost her job. Lonely and sad after her failed marriage, she started to write poetry. At school, she had been talented at writing and had won several academic honors. Shortly after she met Clyde Barrow in 1930, he was sent to Eastham Prison Farm for two years. Bonnie decided to wait for him. She dreamed of the romantic adventures they would share when he was released.

The Barrow Gang

After he left jail in February 1932, Clyde formed a gang. Bonnie had waited for him and now joined in his life of crime.

Bonnie was soon in trouble. On April 19, 1932, the gang tried to rob a hardware store in Kaufman, Texas. The robbery went wrong. Bonnie and another member of the gang, Ralph Fults, were caught. Fults was tried and sent to prison. Bonnie spent a few months in the county jail. However, she was not indicted. Instead, she was freed and warned to stay out of trouble. But she did not listen to the warning.

First murders

The Barrow Gang may have committed their first murder on April 30, 1932. Storekeeper J. N. Bucher was killed accidentally after he had opened his

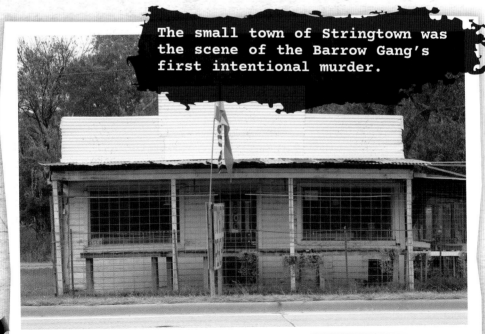

The small town of Stringtown was the scene of the Barrow Gang's first intentional murder.

Storekeeper Howard Hall was killed because Clyde thought he was too slow to hand over the money from his cash register.

safe for the gang. The next murder came in August 1932. Clyde was with gang members Raymond Hamilton and Ross Dyer. They went to a barn dance just over the Texas state line in Stringtown, Oklahoma. The three men were drinking beer when the local sheriff and his deputy approached them. Clyde and Hamilton fired on both men. Deputy Eugene Moore was killed. Sheriff C. G. Maxwell was seriously injured.

Another killing soon followed. This time the victim was Howard Hall. He was a storekeeper in Sherman, Texas. Clyde shot him dead while robbing the store. Hall was not quick enough to hand over the $28 he had in his cash register.

THE FORD MODEL V-8

The Barrow Gang stole cars to get around. Clyde was a skilled driver who could drive up to 1,000 miles (1,600 km) at a time. His favorite car was the Ford V-8, which was known for its comfort, speed, and good handling. Clyde is said to have written to carmaker Henry Ford praising the V-8.

15

Clyde's favorite car was the Ford Model V-8. Clyde liked to steal cars that were fast enough to outrun the police.

Christmas Day murder

In December 1932, Clyde recruited a new member to his gang. William Daniel (W. D.) Jones was a family friend. He was only 16 years old at the time, and admired Clyde. On Christmas Eve Jones left Dallas with Bonnie and Clyde.

The next day, they were in Temple, Texas. Clyde tried to steal a Model A Ford Roadster. The driver was Doyle Johnson. He was a new father on his way home for Christmas dinner with his young family. Johnson tried to stop Clyde from stealing his car but Clyde shot him dead.

Another killing

Two weeks later, Clyde shot and killed Deputy Sheriff Malcolm Davis in Tarrant County. The Barrow Gang had walked into a trap the deputy had set for a criminal friend of Clyde. The friend was thought to have carried out a bank robbery. The sheriff was waiting in the house when Clyde showed up and shot him. The gang was now wanted for killing five people.

YOUNG GANG MEMBER

W. D. Jones was part of the Barrow Gang from Christmas 1932 until September 1933. When he felt the police were closing in on the gang, he tried to quit. Clyde stopped him from leaving, but Jones eventually stole a car and escaped. He later served six years in prison for his part in the gang's crimes.

W. D. Jones quit the gang in September 1933. He said later that he'd had "enough blood."

A Family Affair

Clyde's brother Buck was also an outlaw. He had been sent to jail in 1929. Upon his release he joined the Barrow Gang.

Marvin "Buck" Barrow had been sent to jail for robbery in November 1929. He escaped a few months later and went home to West Dallas. There he married his sweetheart, Blanche Caldwell. She and some of Buck's family convinced him to return to jail and serve the rest of his prison term. Buck was released on March 22, 1933. He and Blanche met up with Bonnie and Clyde and joined the Barrow Gang. The two couples and W. D. Jones moved to an apartment in Joplin, Missouri.

This photograph shows Buck and Blanche while on the run with the gang in 1933.

Suspicious neighbors

For two weeks the gang stayed inside. But their presence was soon noticed by people in the small local community. No one from the apartment went out during the day. People started to wonder who lived there. The gang began to play noisy card games and have parties. Beer had been illegal during the 1920s, but in March 1933 President Franklin D. Roosevelt had made it legal again. One night, during a particularly noisy party, Clyde accidentally fired his rifle. The neighbors immediately contacted the Joplin police department.

OUTLAW'S WIFE

Blanche was an unlikely outlaw's wife. She fell in love with Buck before she knew he was a criminal and did her best to get him to give up his outlaw life. When she failed, she decided to join him. After Buck was released from jail, he was determined to meet up with Clyde, so Blanche joined the gang, too.

The gang ended up hiding from the law in the small town of Joplin, Missouri.

Shootout in Joplin

When the police arrived at the gang's apartment they had no idea that they were about to have a gunfight on their hands.

On April 13, 1933, the police arrived in two cars and approached the apartment. They thought they were simply dealing with a group of noisy people at a drunken party. They called for everyone to come out of the building with their hands up. Instead Clyde and Buck Barrow, Bonnie, and W. D. Jones burst out firing Browning Automatic Rifles. Blanche did not shoot. Instead, she ran out of the building screaming. The police were so shocked and surprised that they did not shoot at her.

On the run

Better armed than the police, the gang shot their way out of the apartment building and past the police. Outside, Bonnie provided covering fire

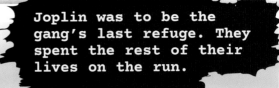

Joplin was to be the gang's last refuge. They spent the rest of their lives on the run.

The apartment still stands on Oakridge Drive in Joplin.

while Clyde, Buck, and W. D. Jones jumped into their car. As they made their getaway, Jones was shot in his side. The gang drove off down the street to pick up Blanche. She had run off to catch her little white dog, which had escaped during the shooting.

Of the five police officers, two were killed and another was seriously injured. The incident became known as the Joplin Massacre. The Barrow Gang had become notorious outlaws.

ARMING THE POLICE

In the 1920s and 1930s, outlaws such as John Dillinger and Clyde Barrow often used submachine guns or automatic rifles. The FBI (Federal Bureau of Investigation) and some police forces began to use the same weapons. They also used armored cars to fight the outlaws. However, most law enforcement agents only carried a shotgun. It was no match for the criminals' weapons.

Nationwide Fame

After the gang fled, the police searched the apartment in Joplin. They found personal documents and two rolls of film.

The personal possessions included Blanche and Buck's wedding certificate and Buck's prison parole papers. There was also a copy of a long poem by Bonnie called "Suicide Sal." Bonnie had written it while she was in jail in spring 1932. The poem told the story of a girl in jail who had been left by her gangster boyfriend. Bonnie's poem was published in many newspapers.

Caught on film

Also in the apartment were two used rolls of camera film. When the pictures were developed, they revealed some of the most famous crime images of all time.

Bonnie pretends to rob Clyde in this photo. It was on one of the rolls of film.

Bonnie wrote her poem "Suicide Sal" in prison in 1932.

The pictures showed Bonnie and Clyde holding weapons and posing for the camera. They were probably taken by W. D. Jones. In one photograph, Bonnie pretends to hold up Clyde with a shotgun. In another, she has her foot on a car bumper. She has a pistol on her hip and a cigar in her mouth. Bonnie was said not to like the picture. The poem and photographs made Bonnie and Clyde famous. Everyone wanted to read about them.

GAINING PUBLICITY

The newswire service had been set up to write news stories that were sent to papers around the country. It helped to make the Barrow Gang front-page news far beyond Texas. Readers were fascinated by the photos of Bonnie and Clyde and by Bonnie's poem. The couple was famous.

Popular Heroes

Many Americans saw Bonnie and Clyde as public heroes. In the years of the Great Depression some people sympathized with the idea of robbing banks.

The effects of the Great Depression left many Americans in poverty. By 1932, 10 million people were out of work. Another 30 million people had very little money. Many turned to minor theft to try to raise money for food. Many of these people also followed the stories of more ambitious robbers.

Men such as "Babyface" Nelson and "Machine Gun" Kelly held up banks in towns throughout the Midwest. They were thieves and murderers, but the public loved to read about them. Many people sympathized with the criminals. They saw the outlaws as fighting against the authorities and the banks that had caused the Great Depression. The public thought they understood why criminals felt they had to follow a life of crime.

Photos of Bonnie and Clyde appear on the front page of a newspaper from El Paso, Texas.

George "Machine Gun" Kelly was an armed robber and kidnapper from Tennessee. He was also seen by many as a public hero.

Crime in the Depression

The nature of crime had changed during the 1930s. Better highways and better maps made it possible for outlaws to travel easily. Criminals often targeted banks in small towns in the Midwest. These banks were not well guarded. Robbers could attack a bank and leave town before the police even knew about it.

PUBLIC ENEMIES

J. Edgar Hoover was the director of the FBI. He did not see criminals as public heroes. He called them public enemies. Hoover made catching famous criminals his priority. By 1935, FBI agents had killed or captured the most famous outlaws of the Great Depression.

Escaping the Law

Photographs of Bonnie and Clyde were on the front pages of every newspaper. They could trust no one and were on the run.

The outlaws did not want to risk staying in tourist parks or motels where they might be recognized. Instead, they camped out or slept in their cars. The gang stayed one step ahead of the police. Clyde stole a new car every week or two. They took their clothes to public laundries for cleaning. When they went to get their clothes, they checked for police activity. If there was any chance of being caught, they left the clothes and bought new ones.

Bonnie's accident

On June 10, 1933, Clyde was driving fast on a deserted highway through a region of Texas called the Panhandle. He ignored signs that a bridge was

This police department WANTED poster used photographs taken by gang members.

F.P.C.29 - NO. 9
26 U 00 6

WANTED FOR MURDER
JOPLIN, MISSOURI

CLYDE CHAMPION BARROW, age 24, 5'7", 130#, hair dark brown and wavy, eyes hazel, light complexion, home West Dallas, Texas. This man killed Detective Harry McGinnis and Constable J.W. Harryman in this city, April 13, 1933.

BONNIE PARKER   CLYDE BARROW   CLYDE BARROW

This man is dangerous and is known to have committed the following murders: Howard Hall, Sherman, Texas; J.N.Bucher, Hillsboro, Texas; a deputy sheriff at Atoka, Okla; deputy sheriff at West Dallas, Texas; also a man at Belden, Texas.

The above photos are kodaks taken by Barrow and his companions in various poses, and we believe they are better for identification than regular police pictures.

Wire or write any information to the

A freight train passes beside a highway in the Texas Panhandle.

out and had to swerve at the last minute. The car crashed down a steep embankment. Clyde and W. D. Jones escaped. Bonnie was trapped inside the car, which burst into flames. Bonnie's screams alerted two local farmers who pulled her from the burning car. They took her to a farm to treat her injuries. A suspicious farmer called the sheriff. The outlaws were forced to flee. They took the sheriff and a deputy hostage but later released them unharmed in Oklahoma.

LIFE-CHANGING INJURIES

Bonnie was seriously injured in the car fire. Her right leg was so badly burned that the bone was visible. She almost died from her injuries. For weeks she was half conscious. After her recovery, her leg was permanently damaged. Walking became difficult for her.

Shootout at the Red Crown

Bonnie was seriously hurt so the gang broke their own rule and took her to a motel to rest and recover. It was a big mistake.

The gang rented two brick cabins joined by garages at the Red Crown Tourist Court in Platte City, Missouri. The locals were suspicious of the new arrivals. Blanche only registered three guests, but the motel owner saw five people going into the cabins. The gang paid for everything with coins. They also taped newspapers over the windows of the cabins.

Toward midnight that evening, July 20, 1933, the local police and reinforcements from Kansas City surrounded the cabins. A gunfight began as the gang ran to their getaway car. Clyde had to

Crime scene investigators at the Red Crown after the shootout.

carry Bonnie to the car, because she was unconscious from her injuries. Clyde's brother Buck was shot in the head and badly wounded.

One more narrow escape

A police car blocked the gang's path. W. D. Jones fired at it until the driver was forced to pull out of the way. The police continued firing as the gang sped off. Bullets shattered the car windows. Pieces of glass flew into Blanche's eyes, badly damaging them. For the outlaws, life on the run was becoming even harder.

DEATH OF BUCK

The shootout at Red Crown was a turning point for the gang. Buck Barrow died a few days later from his injuries after another police shootout at an amusement park in Iowa. Blanche was arrested as she cradled her dying husband. She spent six years in jail. After her release she wrote about her time with the gang.

Blanche under arrest after the shootout with police in Iowa. She was jailed for attempted murder.

Eastham Breakout

Two months after the shootout at Red Crown, Clyde was ready to carry out his threat to attack Eastham Prison Farm.

After their escape from the Red Crown Tourist Court, the remaining members of the gang went into hiding again. Clyde decided the time was right to attack Eastham Prison Farm and free his friend Raymond Hamilton. He hid two revolvers at the edge of the farm's land. Early on January 16, 1934, Hamilton was working near the farm boundary. He and a man named Joe Palmer found the guns. They shot their two guards and escaped. One of the guards later died.

A full car

Clyde was waiting for Hamilton and Palmer with a getaway car. To Clyde's surprise, three other criminals also joined them. Clyde drove

Clyde had wanted to take revenge on Eastham Prison Farm since his imprisonment in 1932.

for 250 miles (400 km), then dropped off two of the men. The third, Henry Methvin, joined the Barrow Gang, along with Hamilton and Palmer.

The prison guard who died was named Major Crowson. After his death, the governor of the Texas prisons, Lee Simmons, was determined to destroy the Barrow Gang. He knew just the man for the job.

HENRY METHVIN

Henry Methvin was serving 10 years in prison for robbery. After he escaped with Hamilton and the others, he joined the Barrow Gang. He committed murders with Clyde. His father later helped the police trap Bonnie and Clyde. No one knows if Henry also helped to give away his friends.

This criminal record card for Henry Methvin was created at the Oklahoma State Penitentiary in 1935.

Frank A. Hamer

The governor of the Texas prisons chose Frank A. Hamer, a former Texas Ranger, to track down Clyde and the Barrow Gang.

Hamer was already famous for catching wanted criminals. His career had started early in the 20th century. Hamer was almost 50 years old when Lee Simmons hired him to hunt down the Barrow Gang. Although the pay was half what Hamer was earning as an officer in the Texas Highway Patrol, Hamer took the pay cut to take the job. He was eager to catch the outlaws who had so far outwitted the law.

Frank A. Hamer (left) discusses plans to catch the outlaws with two other law enforcement officials.

Psychology

Hamer decided the best way to catch Clyde was to try to understand how his mind worked. For 102 days, Hamer followed reports of Clyde's movements from the police. He figured out exactly how the gang moved around. He realized that they traveled in a circle around the Midwest. Clyde crossed in and out of states. That took advantage of the fact that state law forces were not allowed to cross into other states so the gang could not be followed. Hamer figured out that the gang had base cities such as Dallas, Texas, and Joplin, Missouri. They carried out their robberies from these different bases.

MIRIAM "MA" FERGUSON

Lee Simmons was worried that Hamer would not be allowed to hunt the outlaws. The appointment had to be approved by the Texas governor, "Ma" Ferguson. Ferguson was thought to be soft on crime. She had pardoned more than 100 prisoners during her second term. In this case, however, Ferguson allowed Hamer to have the job. She wanted Bonnie and Clyde caught.

Miriam "Ma" Ferguson became the first female governor of Texas in 1925 and was re-elected in 1933.

Texas Rangers

Frank A. Hamer had been a Texas Ranger. The Rangers were formed to guard the border between Mexico and Texas. They were famous for being tough law enforcers.

The Rangers were first formed in 1823. They protected American settlers in what was still the Mexican territory of Texas. At the start of the Texas Revolution in 1835, when the settlers rebelled against the Mexican government, the Texas Rangers became law enforcers for the state. They guarded the frontier during the fighting that led to Texan independence in 1836.

After Texas joined the United States in 1845, the Rangers remained the main law enforcers in Texas. They patrolled the border and fought

Texas Rangers on patrol for the Union Army during the Civil War (1861–1865).

This statue of a Ranger stands outside the Texas Ranger Museum in Waco, Texas.

Native Americans. They also chased outlaws. In 1877 the Rangers caught the outlaw John Wesley Hardin, who had killed 42 people.

The Rangers were civilians. They supplied their own horses and weapons. In remote parts of state, the Rangers were known to take the law into their own hands. By the 1930s, many Texans thought the Rangers were too violent. Frank A. Hamer, for example, had killed at least 80 people. The state started to turn the Rangers into a more conventional police force.

"ONE RIOT, ONE RANGER"

This famous saying is associated with the Texas Rangers after Ranger Captain "Bill" McDonald was sent to Dallas in 1896 to stop an illegal boxing fight. When asked where his backup was, he is alleged to have said there was only one fight so only one Ranger was needed.

Grapevine Killings

The Grapevine Killings on Easter Sunday, 1934, marked a turning point. Popular sympathy for the Barrow Gang disappeared.

On April 1, 1934, near Grapevine, Texas, the gang were approached by two highway patrolmen. Henry Methvin began firing at them and Clyde Barrow joined in. Troopers Edward Wheeler and H. D. Murphy were killed. Methvin later claimed that Bonnie had also taken part in the shootings. He said she had stood laughing over the bodies. This was not true, but the public believed it. Public outrage grew when Murphy's fiancée went to his funeral wearing her wedding dress. The Highway Patrol and the Texas governor's office offered a combined reward of $2,000 for the bodies of Bonnie, Clyde, and the Barrow Gang.

A price on their heads

Five days after the Grapevine murders, Clyde and Methvin killed

A Fort Worth newspaper reports the killings of the two policemen near Grapevine.

MORNING **FORT WORTH STAR-TELEGRAM** COMPLETE MARKET

A FORT WORTH OWNED NEWSPAPER

TWO STATE HIGHWAY PATROL OFFICERS SLAIN AS THEY APPROACH AUTO CLOSE TO GRAPEVINE

TURKEY WILL TURN INSULL OVER TO U.S.

Crest of Hill on Crossroad Where Pair Were Killed

BARROW AND RED-HEADED WOMAN BELIEVED TO HAVE SHOT DOWN POLICEMEN

CHRISTIANS AT CHRIST'S TOMB

MAIL ROBBERY CASE NEAR JURY

Trammell Is Captured In Barn Near Coleman

DOUBLE KILLING SEEN BY COUPLE

WOMAN TELLS OF ABDUCTION

New Presidential Retreat Has Had Varied History

36

WE THE PEOPLE OF THE STATE OF
TEXAS
ACKNOWLEDGE AND THANK TROOPERS
EDWARD BRYAN WHEELER
AND
H. D. MURPHY
FOR THE GREAT SACRIFICE THEY
MADE TO KEEP THE PUBLIC SAFE.

TROOPERS WHEELER AND MURPHY
WERE SHOT TO DEATH EASTER SUNDAY,
APRIL 1, 1934 NEAR THIS SITE ON
WEST DOVE ROAD BY THE INFAMOUS
CRIMINALS BONNIE PARKER AND
CLYDE BARROW. WHEELER AND MURPHY
STOPPED THEIR MOTORCYCLES NEAR
PARKER AND BARROW'S CAR, THINKING
A MOTORIST NEEDED ASSISTANCE. WHEN
THEY APPROACHED, THEY WERE SHOT.

THEIR EFFORTS WILL STAND THE
TEST OF TIME.

MAY GOD BLESS THEIR SOULS.

ERECTED 1996

This memorial to the two dead troopers stands on the site of the Grapevine killings.

60-year-old police constable Cal Campbell outside Commerce, Oklahoma. The town's police chief, Percy Boyd, was also kidnapped by the gang. They later released him unharmed. Boyd had seen Campbell's murder. Although he had not learned Methvin's name, he gave the authorities evidence to issue warrants for the arrests of Clyde Barrow and Bonnie Parker. Time was running out for them.

A TURNING POINT

The Grapevine killings marked a low point in the public image of Bonnie and Clyde. People felt great sympathy with the two young troopers. Edward Wheeler had only been married for two years. H. D. Murphy was due to marry Marie Tullis 12 days after the murder took place. His fiancée wore her wedding dress to his funeral.

The Net Closes In

After the Grapevine killings, Hamer knew where they would head next. He formed a posse ready to make his move.

Hamer had worked out that the gang moved in a circular pattern along state lines to avoid capture. He also knew they visited their families regularly. He figured out that their next visit was likely to be to Henry Methvin's family in Louisiana.

Betrayed

Hamer made a plan. He ordered a large number of Browning Automatic Rifles and 20 rounds of armor-piercing bullets. He also handpicked a posse of five men who he knew could trust. On May 21, the posse left Texas for Shreveport, Louisiana, where they waited.

Frank A. Hamer (front, right) handpicked his five-man posse.

This car is parked on the isolated road where the outlaws arranged to meet.

Clyde, Bonnie, and Henry Methvin had agreed that they would meet up on an isolated highway in Bienville, Louisiana, close to Methvin's family home. However, Methvin's father, Ivan, had done a deal with Hamer. He told the posse where the outlaws would be and when they were expected to arrive. In return, Hamer had promised that Henry Methvin would be spared the death sentence if he was captured. Everything was set for the fatal ambush.

THE POSSE

Hamer's posse included two men who could identify Bonnie and Clyde. Ted Hinton knew Bonnie from her waitressing days and Bob Alcorn knew Clyde by sight. The other members of the posse were former Texas Ranger Manny Gaul, Sheriff Henderson Jordan from Bienville, Louisiana, and deputy Prentiss Oakley.

Surprise Attack

Early on the morning of May 23, 1934, a car approached the ambush at high speed. It was to be the final shootout.

There were two people inside the car. Clyde Barrow was driving. Bonnie Parker was in the passenger seat. As Clyde sped along the isolated road, he saw Ivan Methvin's truck blocking his path. The truck seemed to have broken down. The posse was hidden in the woods along the side of the road waiting to ambush Bonnie and Clyde.

Shot dead!

What happened next is uncertain. According to some accounts, the posse opened fire as Clyde slowed down to pass the truck. Other accounts

This photograph shows the car riddled with bullet holes after the attack.

state that one of the posse ordered the car to stop. The rest of the posse then opened fire. The firing continued until 150 rounds had been emptied into the car. Clyde and Bonnie were hit many times and killed. Hamer made sure that no one had survived before ordering the attack to stop. Henry Methvin had escaped the ambush. He had hitchhiked to his father's home beforehand.

FAMILY REUNIONS

Bonnie and Clyde made sure they visited their families regularly. Bonnie, in particular, missed her mom and liked to visit. The outlaws' mothers had urged them to surrender many times. After Bonnie and Clyde died, their mothers were both found guilty of helping them. They were each sentenced to 30 days in jail.

A Dallas newspaper reports the killings. Newspaper sales rose steeply.

Legacy

People immediately flocked to the small town of Arcadia. They wanted to see the bodies of the outlaws who had been made famous by the newspapers.

By dusk on the day of the killings, the population of the small Louisiana town of Arcadia had risen from 3,000 to 12,000. The roads into town were blocked. Everyone wanted to see the famous outlaws. They cut off pieces of their hair and clothes as souvenirs.

Separated forever

Bonnie and Clyde had separate funerals. They had asked to be buried together, but the Parker family would not allow this. Bonnie's funeral became a public event. The funeral home was filled with floral tributes. It was said that other

The car in which Bonnie and Clyde died became a tourist attraction in Arcadia.

WARREN BEATTY
FAYE DUNAWAY

THEY'RE YOUNG...
THEY'RE IN LOVE...
AND THEY
KILL PEOPLE

BONNIE AND CLYDE

MICHAEL J. POLLARD · GENE HACKMAN · ESTELLE PARSONS

WRITTEN BY DAVID NEWMAN and ROBERT BENTON · MUSIC BY Charles Strouse · PRODUCED BY WARREN BEATTY · DIRECTED BY ARTHUR PENN · TECHNICOLOR® FROM WARNER BROS.-SEVEN ARTS · RELEASED

The 1967 movie suggested that outlaws lived exciting and romantic lives.

outlaws such as the criminals John Dillinger and "Pretty Boy" Floyd sent flowers. The biggest arrangement of flowers came from the Dallas newspapers. Bonnie's death had helped to increase the number of papers they sold to half a million a day. The newspapers printed another poem by Bonnie, called "The Trail's End."

Since their deaths in 1934, Bonnie and Clyde have been the subject of books and movies. The most famous movie, *Bonnie and Clyde*, was released in 1967. It made the outlaws' lives on the run appear more romantic than they had ever been.

"THE TRAIL'S END"

This is the beginning of Bonnie's poem. She saw the gang as being in the tradition of other outlaws.

You've read the story of Jesse James
of how he lived and died.
If you're still in need;
of something to read,
here's the story of Bonnie and Clyde.
Now Bonnie and Clyde are the
Barrow gang
I'm sure you all have read.
how they rob and steal;
and those who squeal,
are usually found dying or dead.

Rogues' Gallery

During the Great Depression, poverty caused many people to step outside the law. Like Bonnie and Clyde, some criminals became household names.

"Pretty Boy" Floyd (1904–1934)

Charles Arthur Floyd was a bank robber. He got his nickname because he looked young. His gang killed up to 10 police officers. Floyd was popular, however. People saw him as a victim of the Depression. He was shot dead by law enforcement officials.

"Ma" Barker (1873–1935)

Ma Barker's real name was Arizona Barker. She was the mother of several criminals who formed the Barker Gang. Ma Barker ran the gang, which carried out robberies and kidnappings across the Midwest. She was killed in a shootout with the Federal Bureau of Investigation (FBI).

"Machine Gun" Kelly
(1895–1954)

George Francis Kelly got his nickname from his favorite weapon, the Thompson submachine gun. He was an armed robber. His biggest crime was the kidnapping of a businessman in 1933. Kelly was paid a ransom of $200,000. He was caught that same year and spent the rest of his life in jail.

"Baby Face" Nelson
(1908–1934)

George Nelson got his nickname because of his small size and young appearance. He was a bank robber who worked with John Dillinger. Nelson was responsible for killing a number of policemen. The FBI shot him dead.

John Dillinger
(1903–1934)

John Dillinger became the FBI's Public Enemy Number One in June 1934. His gang robbed 24 banks. He was said to be very violent, although he was only known to have killed one police officer. Dillinger was on the run for a year before he was shot dead by FBI agents as he was leaving a movie theater in Chicago.

Glossary

Accomplice A person who helps someone commit a crime.

Confederacy The country set up by the Southern states that left the United States in 1861.

Economic Boom A period when there is a lot of business activity and sales are high.

Embankment A bank of earth that carries a road or railroad over low ground.

Flapper A fashionable young woman in the 1920s.

Great Depression A long period of low global economic activity in the 1930s.

Indicted Charged with a crime and ordered to go to court.

Kidnapped Seized and held someone against their will.

Massacre The indiscriminate killing of many people.

Notoriety Fame gained by bad or evil actions.

Parole The release of a prisoner early for their good behavior.

Posse A group of citizens helping a sheriff.

Prison Term The period of time for which a criminal is sent to prison.

Reinforcements Extra personnel who increase the numbers of a force.

Reputation How someone or something is judged by the general public.

Revolvers Pistols with a revolving chamber to hold the bullets.

Roadster A sporty, open-top or convertible automobile with two seats.

Romantic Associated with an idealized and perfect view of reality.

Rounds Individual bullets fired by a gun.

Stock Market A place where people buy shares in companies in the hopes of making money.

Warrants Papers authorizing the police to make an arrest.

Further Resources

Books

Blumenthal, Karen. *Bonnie and Clyde: The Making of a Legend.* Viking Books for Young Readers, 2018.

Buckley, James. *Bonnie and Clyde* (History's Worst). Aladdin, 2018.

Hinton, Ted and Larry Grove. *Ambush: The Real Story of Bonnie and Clyde.* Eakin Press, 2020.

Smith, Elliott. *Focus on The Great Depression.* Lerner, 2023.

Websites

www.fbi.gov/about-us/history/famous-cases/bonnie-and-clyde
Bonnie and Clyde's crimes and the story of the campaign to stop them from the website of the Federal Bureau of Investigation.

www.biography.com/people/bonnie-parker-9542045
A biography of Bonnie Parker from Biography.com, with a video.

www.biography.com/people/clyde-barrow-229532
The Biography.com page and video about Clyde Barrow.

www.crimemuseum.org/crime-library/robberies/bonnie-clyde/
Pages from the Crime Museum in Washington, D.C., which was opened in 2008 as an educational resource for crime history, forensic science, and law enforcement.

www.cinetropic.com/janeloisemorris/commentary/bonn&clyde/wdjones.html
A reprinted version of an interview given by W. D. Jones in 1968 about his life with Bonnie and Clyde.

Publisher's note to educators and parents: Our editors have carefully reviewed these websites to ensure that they are suitable for students. Many websites change frequently, however, and we cannot guarantee that a site's future contents will continue to meet our high standards of quality and educational value. Be advised that students should be closely supervised whenever they access the Internet.

INDEX